MARK HARRISON'S
DREAMLANDS

MARK HARRISON'S
DREAMLANDS

TEXT BY LISA TUTTLE

Paper Tiger

<u>TO MY MOTHER AND FATHER</u>

TITLE PAGE
The Garden of Eden (Dragon's World, 1983)

Paper Tiger
An imprint of Dragon's World Ltd
Limpsfield
Surrey RH8 0DY
Great Britain

First printed in 1990
Reprinted 1992

British Library Cataloguing in Publication Data
Harrison, Mark
Mark Harrison's dreamlands.
1. English illustrations. Harrison, Mark
I. Title II. Tuttle, Lisa
741.942
ISBN 1 85028 133 5 (*Hardback*)
ISBN 1 85028 132 7 (*Limpback*)

EDITOR Michael Downey
DESIGNER Bob Gordon
ART DIRECTOR Dave Allen
EDITORIAL DIRECTOR Pippa Rubinstein

Typeset by Dragon's World Ltd
Printed in Singapore

■ CONTENTS

PAINTER
OF DREAMS

Mark Harrison dreams of his pictures long before he actually paints them. He is haunted by vivid, colourful dreams which, when he wakes, he is eager to paint. Some of his changes in technique, style and subject matter over the years have been prefigured by dreams in which he foresaw his new work, as if by visiting the future.

Other artists have had this experience, perhaps more than admit to it. The paintings of Bosch, de Chirico, and Magritte are reminiscent of dream landscapes; Blake claimed to have been taught a new technique of engraving while he slept, and the Surrealists placed great emphasis on the dream-state as a means of access to the non-logical springs of art.

As an illustrator, however, a commercial rather than 'fine' artist, Harrison cannot simply paint whatever he sees in his dreams, and he is aware of a contradiction inherent in the way he works. He says: 'Because my paintings are commissioned the ideas come from the outside, whereas dreams are internal, and very personal. So I can't really use the ideas from my dreams in my work. The way I like to do things has been influenced by my dreams, but not the subject matter . . . as far as I can tell. Of course, it's hard to know. The mind does store things away, and an image from a dream may pop up in a painting years later, when there's a place for it. If the paintings I dream about really do come from the future, then maybe now I'm painting the things I dreamed of five or ten years ago. But I can't always be sure that I remember the paintings in my dreams as they really were.'

Mark Harrison was born February 27, 1951 ('Pisces, Aquarius rising with a Scorpio moon, for the information of any old hippies out there.') in Leicester, a city he dismisses with a sigh as 'Nowhere. I won't say any more about it.' For someone who has always felt a powerful attraction to the exotic, and a yearning for other lands, a childhood spent in an ugly industrial town in the English Midlands must have been a major disappointment. He escaped as soon as he could, to art college in Nottingham (1969–71), followed by a postgraduate course at Wimbledon (1972–73). Living in the London area he began taking his portfolio around to book publishers, with the result that he got his first commission – a cover for Thornton Wilder's *Theophilus North*, published by Penguin – while still at college. This was all the encouragement he needed to set up

Putting Out
(Sphere Books, 1988)

as a freelance illustrator, rather than looking for a job as most of his fellow students did.

> 'I was lucky, at first, that editors liked my work and commissioned more, but when something turned out well it was often a fluke, and the next two or three covers wouldn't be any good at all. I did a lot of nondescript stuff at the beginning. In fact, a group of artists once had a turkey competition for the worst published work, and I won hands down, first and third prizes. Really, some of the stuff I did was appalling. So it's not surprising that I never had a volume of work coming in. It was all in dribs and drabs, and I'd be signing on half the time, then signing off when I got another commission. Finally, by 1979, I'd had enough. I was tired of seeing my friends going off on holidays while I was debating over whether or not I could afford a jar of jam this week. So I gave it all up and became a clerk. Yes, I was a Kelly Girl.
>
> And I loved it, at the start. It was great having money. But there was no future in it, it was all temporary work, with no chance to get ahead. So I had to reconsider what I was doing, and what I could do.'

Harrison began to paint again, this time for himself. 'I didn't consider the market, I just thought about the images I wanted to paint, and for once my mind was full of ideas. I don't know where they came from, maybe from my dreams, but they were there, and I did about ten paintings and put together a portfolio. I went to a fortune-teller at about this time, and he said there would be a man in the West End who would help me, so,' Harrison laughs, 'as I was looking for an agent, after a few more throws of the Tarot cards, I chose a man with a West End address! Very haphazard, my life, but it was a good move. It worked out. I think that break really focused things for me – what a good idea it is for everyone to give up illustration for a year or two! It clears the mind and gives you money to spend.'

Since breaking into the American market as a cover artist Harrison has had more money – and, more importantly, time – to spend. An artist working solely for British publishers, with no other source of income, can't afford to take too long over any one painting – 'you almost have to become a machine, churning them out,' he says. Now, though, he is able to con-

**The Two Deaths
of Señora Puccini**
(Viking Books, 1987)

centrate on only two paintings a month, and the additional time
and care he takes shows. The days of winning 'turkey' compe-
titions, like the days of temporary office jobs, are now happily
gone for good.

Today Mark Harrison lives in Hove, on the south coast of
England, within sight of the sea. The many windows of his top
floor flat bring the light and colours of the changeable sky into
the room where he works. Intricate wooden carvings of gods
and monsters, souvenirs of his travels, are the first things to
catch the visitor's eye. Music from Africa or Bali, house
music, or even his own musical experiments (he is the percus-
sionist with a local group called Gamelanadingdong) fills the air
while he leans over his worktable, turning the pictures inside
his head into colourful dreams he can share.

1 DREAMING OF EVE

THE WOMAN WHO HAUNTS Mark Harrison's dreams represents an ancient and powerful archetype. She is a symbol of fertility, the human embodiment of the goodness of nature. Surrounded by flowers, vines and leafy plants, her hair growing in tendrils, interwoven with leaves or adorned with fruit, she is at home in the wild as civilized man can never be. Infinitely desirable, she cannot be captured or tamed and can never really be known. She is always solitary, self-contained, and mysterious. She may have company, she may be partnered by lizard, snake, spider, bird or some other familiar spirit, but she is never seen with a man. She is not part of a crowd, but the very first woman, Eve. Rather than unique individuals, all the women he paints seem to be one woman, aspects of a primeval goddess known by many names.

He calls her the 'jungle woman' and admits to being obsessed by the image of a woman in lush, tropical surroundings. 'I don't know why women and undergrowth should be such a passion of mine, but all my life I've been drawn to the exotic. To me the sight of bridesmaids with flowers twined in their hair is wonderfully romantic. Maybe it's an obvious romantic image, a woman with fruit and flowers in her hair, a cliché, really – but I rather like clichés. The point about a cliché is that it is obvious, so it communicates something very quickly, and everyone knows what you're talking about. So if you take a clichéd idea but do it really well, you can have a very effective painting.'

But while he does occasionally go for the straightforward romantic view of a young woman with blossom in her hair, as in *Eve: Her Story* (page 15), Harrison usually favours something darker, even rather threatening, as decoration for his exotic women: one has her innocence guarded by a watchful panther and a powerful snake (page 11), another is the languid keeper of a very large and hairy spider (page 7), and one has not fruit or flowers but live snakes framing her face (page 15). The exotic may be romantic, but it is also dangerous – in that mixture lies its powerful allure, as the artist knows very well.

Although he has always liked variety in his work, until recently Harrison has been better known for landscapes in which figures, if they appeared at all, have tended to be fairly small and unimportant, certainly not the centre of attention. In his 'jungle women' paintings not only has the focus of interest

Eva Luna
(Penguin Books, 1989)
'The composition was inspired by a nineteenth-century painting of Eve by Lucien Levy-Dhurmer. The connection between Eve and Eva is obvious, and for the same reason she's holding not an apple but the moon. The artist always spots something that could be better – in this case I have to apologize for the puma.'
MARK HARRISON

shifted to one main figure, but the exotic landscape itself has moved in closer as it becomes personal adornment. Harrison is aware that he is taking a risk, because figures have always been his weak point. Although he is now spending a lot more time and effort trying to improve his figure painting there are occasional lapses; not even the decorative fruits and flowers or the dramatic, almost filmic lighting can disguise the fact that there is something distinctly odd about the two breasts of Señ-ora Puccini (page 9), for example.

But this is something he is determined to correct: 'I was happy to do a lot of landscapes in the past, because I was good at it, but times have changed, and there are other things I want to do. Before I can paint the pictures I know are in me I have to improve my figure painting. One important reason I have been able to get more into figure work during the past two years is because I've been using models, and taking my own pho-tographs, rather than simply using found references. Now that I can afford to take more time on each picture – because commissions from American publishers mean I'm being paid more and don't have to produce so many every month – and now that my own standards are so much higher, I'm sure I will get better. Practise makes perfect, after all.' He laughs, because this is a cliché, but like many clichés it is true.

Even though he often uses his own favourite model (whose interesting face is recognizable in pages 9, 11 and 19) the influence of the works of other artists is perhaps more obvious in these portraits than elsewhere. Illustrator Tom Adams (whose own slight influence on Harrison can be seen in chapter three) has commented on the 'perfectly legitimate practice' of an illustrator occasionally 'to borrow the clothes of well known artists; indeed it is not altogether unknown in the realms of the so called Fine Arts,' yet it is obvious that Harri-son's occasional 'borrowings' from the masters do not lead to imitations, but rather to something quite original.

For example, Harrison's painting for the cover of *Eva Luna* (page 11) was, without being a copy, quite clearly inspired by a nineteenth-century French painting of Eve by Lucien Levy-Dhurmer, as a comparison of the pose held by the woman in each will show. Harrison was pleased to be able to echo the book's title so neatly: 'Eva is Eve and Luna is moon – so here is Eve in a classic pose, even the snake is there lurk-

Stranger in the Forest
(Sphere Books, 1989)

Points of Departure
(Bantam Books, USA, 1989)

LEFT **The Taking of Agnes**
(Sphere Books, 1985)
'The girl in this picture should not be spotted immediately. Some people look at the jungle and don't see her at all, which pleases me although, since I put her there, her presence is blindingly obvious to me.'
MARK HARRISON

ing behind her, watching. But instead of the apple she's holding the moon – an impossible image, which gives it the oddness I like.'

For the cover of *Eve: Her Story* (page 15) Harrison looked for inspiration to the work of another turn-of-the-century artist, Gustav Klimt. Klimt's *Nuda Veritas* of 1899 is a tall, thin painting framed in gold and features a naked woman with flowers in her hair and snake uncoiling around her ankles. This time, it was the physical composition of the painting, the panel effect and the device of the gold frame, frequently used by Klimt, which appealed to Harrison. 'I liked the idea of strips, or panels – it seemed to me a nice way of dealing with the restraints of the standard book cover. Books do tend to force paintings into the same shape all the time, so I like to find ways whenever I can of breaking it up and using the space differently.'

He used a similar compositional approach to his cover for

another novel by the same author, *Glasshouses* (page 15). In this case, the metallic frame and inset was not gold but silver, and for the side panels he tried an experiment.

> 'This was a real heart-in-the-mouth one! The book was about glass-blowing, and colours running through glass, and I thought how great it would be to get that effect of coloured Venetian glass, quite literally, on the cover. So first I did the painting of the woman, and the Lakeland country background, then I marked it off and covered it in a soup of acrylic medium, which is milky when wet but goes clear when it dries. I completely covered it with the medium and then put the colour in – pure colour, red and yellow – and I blew on it, just blew it up the page, and let it dry with no idea what it was going to turn out like. Fortunately, it worked, and I got the almost three-dimensional look in places that I was after.'

For the cover of *The Marianne Trilogy* (page 16), Harrison was inspired not by one particular painting, but by similarities of atmosphere and approach to be found in the works of both Giorgio de Chirico and Paul Delvaux. 'I think de Chirico might even be mentioned in the novel,' he recalled. 'And the atmosphere of the book, which I wanted to express in my painting, is very weird, nightmarish in the way that de Chirico and Delvaux paintings are, full of deserted streets and the repeated figure of a woman. So that seemed the right style to use for that feeling.'

Another discernible influence on Harrison's portrait painting is Hollywood – not the films, but the highly-stylized, carefully posed and lit glamour shots and publicity photos taken of movie stars in the 1930s and 40s. Lighting, and the effects of light and shadow in creating a mood is a perpetual interest, a problem he approaches afresh in every painting, of course, but his present fascination with what he calls 'Hollywood lighting' is most noticeable in some of the pictures in this section. His success in making use of a photographic technique developed in black and white for his own full-colour paintings can be seen particularly in the striking highlights of the upturned face on *Glasshouses*, in the strips of shadow cast by plants across the woman hiding in *The Taking of Agnes* (page 12), in the use of light in *Points of Departure* (page 13), and, perhaps most

Eve: Her Story
(Sphere Books, 1985)

Glasshouses
(Sphere Books, 1988)

obviously, although the woman's Hollywood glamour pose is perhaps less successful than the very beautiful play of light and shadow against flesh, in *The Two Deaths of Señora Puccini* (page 9). In *Memories and Hallucinations* (page 17) Harrison carries the use of concealing shadow to an unusual but very effective extreme to highlight the author's obsession with his mother's smile by making that smile practically her only visible feature.

Photography is an important inspiration to Harrison, although he finds the actual copying of references tedious and to be avoided whenever possible. He prefers to be influenced by photographs in much the way that he is influenced by other works of art, looking at them and letting them work on his imagination. Travel books and other non-fiction, heavily illustrated books, are a favourite recreation, and he says that a large part of his pleasure in travelling abroad is in taking pictures of the things he sees.

The Marianne Trilogy
(Corgi Books, 1989)
'I wanted the picture to feel like a dream, to have the atmosphere of a nightmare in the way that paintings by de Chirico and Delvaux – two very obvious influences on the style – do. It was also an excuse for me to try out a combination of red and purple, purple being my favourite colour.'
MARK HARRISON

Memories and Hallucinations
(Sphere Books, 1989)

**The Gate to
Women's Country**
(Corgi Books, 1990)
*'This is a good example of the
direction my work is currently
taking, the way that figurative
and landscape painting are
coming together. The
publishers didn't want
something that looked like the
standard fantasy cover for this
book, so the landscape is very
much in the background. I
took my inspiration from
Maxfield Parrish in the use of
two types of light: an inner
light from an unknown source
and, from outside, the golden
light of early evening
illuminating the rich blue sky.
In keeping with the title I had
wanted to put a gate behind
the foreground figure but you
can't see much through a gate,
so it's become more of a
window.'*
MARK HARRISON

2 THROUGH THE BEDROOM WINDOW

ASLEEP, THE DREAMER'S eyes are closed, the better to see an inner vision. And the eyes, the windows of the soul, may be represented in dreams as the windows of a building, through which reality is glimpsed.

Some artistic obsessions run deep and last for years, if not a lifetime. Mark Harrison's passion for 'jungle women' is one of these. But his use of windows as a recurring motif, although he refers to it casually as an obsession, is better described as a passing fancy, a personally satisfying solution to the challenge posed by a commission for a series of covers for the Abacus edition of Alison Lurie's novels.

'The idea for that series of covers came quite quickly – if you can call it an idea,' he says. 'The sort of ideas I have are all visual, not thought out, just mental images. Usually it is something quite simple, something to do with a contrast, or with the lighting. The image itself is almost less important that the way you light it, the colours you use, and the composition. So if you can call that an idea . . . that's where it starts.'

Windows were a useful device to give the books an identity in common because they could be used without incongruity on a variety of different texts, while at the same time the possible variations on that theme – as to the type of window, the building, the scenery outside as well as the scene within – are practically endless.

Another common link between the different covers is provided by the formal composition, repeated in each painting, of a centred rectangular shape framed on each side in a way that recalls Harrison's use of panels on the Penelope Farmer covers (pages 14, 15 and 48). Having established this continuity, Harrison then felt free to play around with and alter the meaning of his chosen subject. In the last two paintings in this series (page 22) he has reversed the basic idea of his window. Instead of something opening inward, revealing the story within to an outsider (as in pages 21 and 23), the window is seen from within, of no more importance than the wall serving as a backdrop to the subject. Rather than revealing an inside story, the window offers only a glimpse of an uninteresting outside, some trees or a pale seascape. For these two books it is as if the cover itself has become the window, a pane of glass through which the reader peers at the story. Harrison pushes the association of life-novel-window-painting even further for

The Nowhere City
(Sphere Books, 1985)
'Take a good look through the window at the scene inside, available here for the first time. After I had finished the painting the publishers decided that leg was too rude for a classy book cover, so they blotted it out.'
MARK HARRISON

**The Truth About
Lorin Jones**
(Sphere Books, 1988)

Only Children
(Sphere Books, 1989)

The Truth About Lorin Jones (page 22) by placing a painting (the subject of the title is a painter) in the central position usually occupied by the window. However, he pointed out that for all his care in positioning the windows and the painting absolutely dead-centre, the cover painting for *The Truth About Lorin Jones* was printed off centre.

Harrison's 'window phase' overlapped with a period during which he became fascinated with reproducing different textures, creating visual differences which the eye can almost feel, despite the glossy surface common to all printed reproductions. This is something he still likes to do whenever possible, adding depth and visual interest by using paint as a sculptural medium to recreate the texture of a tree branch, or of rough, pitted stone. To achieve the rough grain of weathered, painted wood on the outside of a house, for example, he used acrylic paint, roughed up the surface very slightly with a toothbrush, let it dry, and then airbrushed it at a very low angle. The result is best seen in the original painting, where the touch of the fingertips confirms the textured look, but the final printed image, although glossier, is still effective. The look of light and shadow on grained wood is subtle and almost photographic in its realism.

'Acrylics are great for that; you can build textures up really quickly with acrylics, and I do quite a lot of that,' says Harrison. For this and several other reasons Harrison works these days almost entirely in acrylics. The story of how he came to do so combines, like so much else in his life, dreams, practical necessity, and pure chance. It might never have happened at all if he had not looked through a window at the right time.

Foreign Affairs
(Sphere Books, 1985)

'I began by using crayon and water colours for the first covers I did, but I was told they didn't reproduce very well and that I should move to gouache, which gives much more solid colours. But I found gouache really hard to work with because it dries so quickly so I moved to alkyd paint, which is sort of halfway between acrylic and oil and which stays wet long enough that you can do things with it. I still like to use alkyd for clouds – you get a much nicer, fuzzier effect – and at one time I was doing a lot of cloudscapes. But working in alkyds was time consuming, having to wait a day for it to dry between coats, and I also felt a bit restricted in the range of colours. I was having dreams in the most amazing colours, and I'd wake up thinking, wow, if only I could get those bright colours in my work!

I was living in Richmond at that time, and as I was walking along the road one day I looked into a window of a house and I saw an illustrator working there in the window. I was going on past, but then I thought, why not say hello? So I knocked on the door and introduced myself. He turned out to be a guy called Mick Brownfield, well known in advertising illustration, and he invited me in. He was using acrylics, and started telling me how great they were – it was just what I'd been looking for. You get nice, strong colours, it dries very quickly, and if you make a mistake or want to build up textures you can go over it again very easily. Great stuff. When I'd started using it I knew then I was at least one step closer to the colours I saw in my dreams.'

Imaginary Friends
(Sphere Books, 1986)

The Brothel on Rosenstrasse

(New English Library, 1983)
'I am told that the author Michael Moorcock thought this cover was 'mustard' – which apparently means 'really good' in his language. When I painted it I had just switched to using acrylics and I was experimenting with textures. I suspect this was also the one which started my window fetish. It's a very atmospheric book, and I tried to capture some of its rich, decadent feeling. The ruined skyline reflected in the window, however, doesn't work as well as I had hoped.'
MARK HARRISON

3 DAYLIGHT NIGHTMARES

WHERE DOES A COVER illustration come from? In an ideal situation Harrison will find that reading the book triggers an immediate inspiration, that the demands of the job mesh happily with his own inner compulsions in a painting which satisfies both artistically and commercially. What kind of book it is does not matter. He feels no preference as to fiction or non-fiction, mystery, contemporary novel or fantasy epic: 'I use the books as excuses to do pictures,' he says.

Obviously, the cover does have to reflect the book's nature, so the first step in starting a new job is to read the book. Usually the book comes with a more or less specific brief from the publisher. 'Sometimes they have certain details that must be included, because they are part of the plot. More often they have a vague idea – for example, a soft, pretty landscape for a fantasy, or something darker and vaguely menacing – but sometimes they just ask me to see what I can come up with. Occasionally they don't know what they want at all. That's the worst, because then I end up spending quite a lot of time on it, and a lot of that is wasted time in the end. I think I work best when there's some enthusiasm behind me – not necessarily for my own work, although of course that's nice, but actually for the book itself.'

'I often prefer a fairly tight brief, where they know what they want, because it saves me having to think too much about it. It's always wonderful to come up with an original idea but, frankly, I do too many covers to be able to think up something great every time. But provided I can vary it (doing something pretty and romantic one month, something weird the next) then what I prefer is to be given as full a brief as possible, but also the freedom to explore my own obsessions and to try something new. That makes it a lot more fun . . . but I probably shouldn't say "fun", should I? That's the wrong word – I'm talking about my life's work, after all!

I like the sense of involvement I get working with books. In advertising work you tend to be following a very precise, specific brief, which is never your idea in the first place. They aren't hiring a specific artist, they're buying my technique. Whereas in publishing, if they want me, it's because they actually want my ideas too, and they'll let me stretch myself, and try something new.'

The Glasshouse
(Sphere Books, 1987)

Having read the book, Harrison usually knows the feeling that he wants to aim for in the cover. The next question is how to translate that feeling into images. Usually the answer is in the book itself, and sometimes his response to the book is such that he has the idea immediately, as soon as he has finished reading, if not before. At other times he has to go looking for a 'trigger', usually by leafing through some of his many art or photographic reference books, sometimes because of something he sees by chance when watching television or wandering around Brighton. And sometimes, he says, 'I can't think of anything at all. I simply have to go to work with what I have, and hope that hard work will produce something interesting in the end.'

An example of a cover idea which came immediately was the one for *Only Children* by Alison Lurie (page 22). 'I knew straight away, as soon as I'd read it, what I would do. It's a book about relationships between adults, but viewed through the eyes of children, and I thought: teddy bears, watching something they shouldn't be watching. And you see, there they are, as if saying "Oh, I can't look" but peeking out from behind their paws . . .

'*The Opium General* (page 39), however, took me ages and ages to get to. It seems like a very simple idea, very obvious now, and I wanted a very simple idea, but getting that simple idea took me a couple of weeks of racking my brain. After the first few days of desperation I just had to leave it and hope that when I got back to it again something would trigger an inspiration . . . And eventually something did: the perfect, simple, obvious idea of a general made of opium smoke.'

When Sphere published *A Taste for Death* and decided to repackage all the rest of P.D. James' novels in the same style, Harrison's brief from the art director was, as he recalls it, a fairly loose one. Because these were detective stories, he inherited the idea of a slightly surreal still-life, a pictorial gathering of clues which had become the convention for that genre following Tom Adams' ground-breaking and extremely popular covers for Agatha Christie.

'There's an inherent challenge in any series, in coming up with something similar yet different for each cover, especially where all the books tend to be a bit alike. Although I did enjoy doing them, there was some difficulty in keeping them from

Innocent Blood
(Sphere Books, 1987)

A Taste for Death
(Sphere Books, 1986)

looking too much the same. At least three of them have almost the same setting, most of them seem to take place in the autumn, and they're all quite dark, with a certain amount of psychological horror in them. One visual link I used to connect them was the presence of blood – there's blood in all of them.' And although the blood is in the obvious place, drooling from the open mouth of the corpse on *Cover Her Face* (page 34), in most of the other paintings the presence of blood adds a surreal touch to what otherwise might be straightforward realism: blood speckled like drops of dew on the pink petals of a rose in *Shroud for a Nightingale* (page 35); the tear, gleaming red as it rolls from the eye of a child (page 28); trickling from a crack in a dummy's skull (page 35); and, perhaps strangest of all, particularly sinister because so inexplicable, the blood that seeps like resin from the opium poppy on the cover of *The Black Tower*. For that matter who, or what, inflicted those evil curved scratches, and what is such a sinister plant doing in an English churchyard anyway?

For the most effective covers, their eerie emotional power should be sought not in the author's logical plot, but in almost prerational connections made by the mind of the artist, where not reason but feeling rules.

'I did my usual thing of trying to fit images to the titles, Harrison explains, 'although sometimes I had to use a bit of lateral thinking. Sometimes you can't follow the details given in the book too closely; sometimes the written ideas don't work visually and you have to come up with something else that does. For example, in the last one I did there's no statue in the garden of *An Unsuitable Job for a Woman*, but as I didn't want to portray the heroine of the book I came up with the idea of incorporating a statue on the cover.

'Some of the details on some of the covers were drawn from life – or should I say death? That's the remains of my lunch on *A Taste for Death* (page 29) – except for the blood, of course! – and the dummy on two of them is a tailor's dummy which I have in the other room.'

A word which comes up often in any conversation with Mark Harrison about his work is atmosphere. 'Atmosphere is, to me, the most important thing about a picture. There is always some specific atmosphere that I'm trying to create, whether it's exotic and dangerous, or the uneasy feeling that a

An Unsuitable Job for a Woman
(Sphere Books, 1987)

LEFT **A Choice of Nightmares**
(Sphere Books, 1987)
'Here I was trying to get the effect of something seen through water. It was an interesting technical experiment and, even though I don't think the break-up of reflections really works, at least I like the leaves. The romantic feeling comes entirely from me and is not the mood of the book which is about a child murder and actually very sad.'
MARK HARRISON

good mystery story should arouse, no matter how familiar and apparently safe the setting is.

'As part of the means of creating atmosphere for the P.D. James covers I decided that each one should have a scene in the background as well as the traditional still-life in the foreground. And I did have fun with these – the woman sitting in the background on *Innocent Blood* (page 28) is actually Margaret Thatcher!'

Colour is another of Harrison's major concerns, in part because it is a way, very powerful and immediate, of creating a mood and of linking (as well as separately identifying) the parts of a series. In addition to using a different colour scheme for each of the P.D. James covers Harrison also tried to play upon unconscious expectations and give the obvious interpretation a twist.

'Blue skies are normally associated with happy things, so I wanted to make a blue sky look menacing. In particular *The Black Tower* might almost be a holiday brochure with the attractive scenery and a happy holiday sky, and yet against that blue, blue sky here we have the poor bloke in his wheelchair about to be pushed off a cliff, and the angel of death waiting to pick him up!

Again, in *Cover Her Face*, the obvious thing would have been to use a red sky, but it occurred to me that a rich, dark blue could also look strange, and be less obvious. Actually, this is one cover which was influenced by a dream – at least, it seems that way to me in retrospect. I dreamed about a huge old gothic house with a very strange sky behind it. A really whacky sky, like nothing I've ever seen before, dark and vivid, with the most incredibly intense colours. The picture isn't quite the same, of course. I toned down the sky quite a bit, but I can definitely see the influence. I was trying to achieve the look and feel of the sky of my dream in that picture, as was the case in the purple sky I used behind the house on *An Unsuitable Job for a Woman*, and maybe some others. It's one of those things I have to keep trying, knowing I can never get it quite right. Anyway the dream gives me something to aim for.'

The Black Tower
(Sphere Books, 1987)

**The Skull Beneath
the Skin**
(Sphere Books, 1987)
'The shape of the skull echoes the shape of the stones around it to imply that more than one body was found on the beach. The letter was typed by my dad, since I'm hopeless with a typewriter, then stuck on and airbrushed to make it seem to be floating in the air.'
MARK HARRISON

A Mind to Murder
(Sphere Books, 1987)

Cover Her Face
(Sphere Books, 1987)

**Death of an
Expert Witness**
(Sphere Books, 1987)

Shroud for a Nightingale
(Sphere Books, 1987)

Driving Through Cuba
(Sphere Books, 1989)

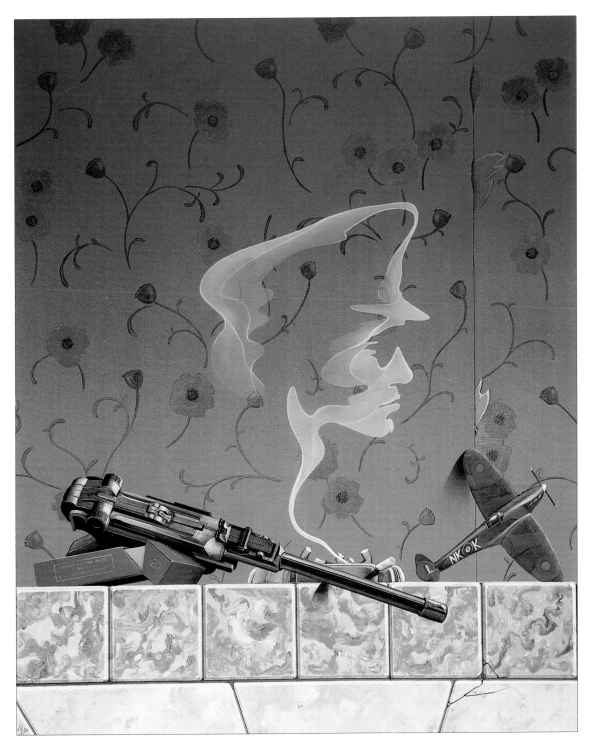

Steel Gods
(Corgi Books, 1989)
*'Believe it or not that's the same
model who posed for* Eva Luna *and*
The Marianne Trilogy. *I told her to
pretend she was a vampire and give
me her meanest look, and this was
the result.'*
MARK HARRISON

The Opium General
(Harrap, 1984)

Waldo/Magic Incorporated
(New English Library, 1986)

RIGHT **Monkey on My Back**
(Sphere Books, 1989)
'This picture was to illustrate the true story of a man who was addicted to opium yet worked as a counsellor for opium and heroin addicts. I still think my original idea of a huge syringe lying on the couch, instead of a second opium-head, would have been more effective.'
MARK HARRISON

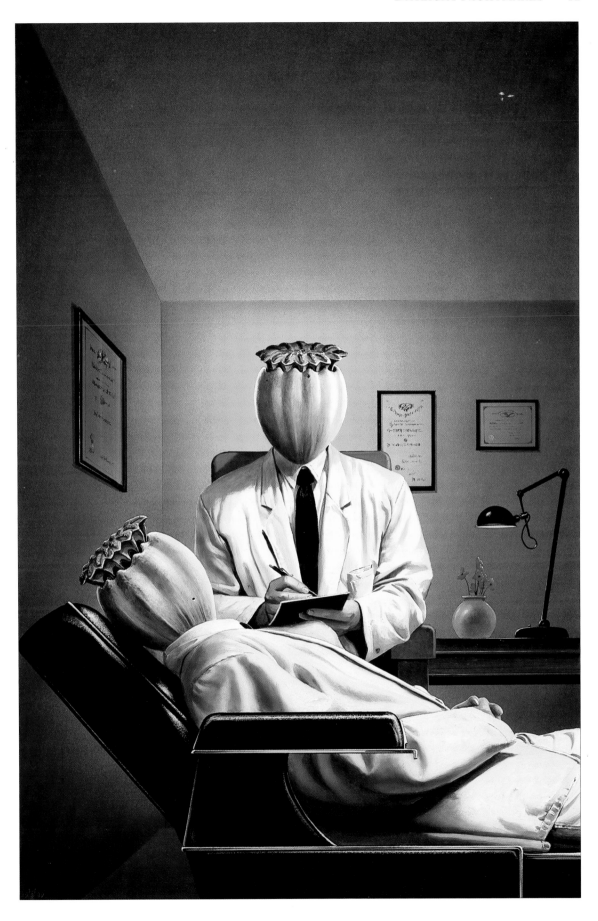

LEFT **Napoleon Disentimed**
(Corgi Books, 1989)

ABOVE **The Mysterious
William Shakespeare**
(Sphere Books, 1988)

Class Porn
(Sphere Books, 1989)
*'Apparently the publishers
have been getting flak from
feminist readers about this
cover but the author, Molly
Hite, wrote to say she thought
it was very much in the spirit
of her feminist spoof of
academia, as well as being
effective marketing.'*
MARK HARRISON

ABOVE **The Power of Silence**
(Corgi Books, 1987)

RIGHT **Sphinx**
(Sphere Books, 1987)

LEFT **Away From Home**
(Sphere Books, 1988)

RIGHT **An Easy Thing**
(Viking Books, USA, 1989)

4 OTHER LANDS, OTHER EYES

AS A CHILD GROWING up in a town he soon considered boring Mark Harrison dreamed of visiting other lands and exploring other ways of life. It wasn't realms of fantasy which attracted him, but the realities of other cultures and landscapes. Like a lot of little boys he imagined being an airline pilot when he grew up, but when his vision turned out to be less than perfect (he wears glasses today) he had to think up another career for himself. Curiously, he was never particularly attracted to art, and never imagined himself as an artist. By chance he saw a television show which made him think he might like to be a geologist working for an oil company. With that plan in mind, he went off to a technical college.

There he found himself with some extra hours to fill, so he chose to do art as an agreeable way of passing the time. He did that well enough. On his tutor's advice he pursued art to both 'O' and 'A' level and finally, still responding to suggestions from his tutor in the same rather haphazard way, still without really imagining he would ever make a living from image-making, he went off to art college.

'The fact that I'm an illustrator is completely accidental, really,' he says, sounding surprised, even slightly apologetic, after nearly two decades spent pursuing this same career. On some level – the place where that little boy imagines himself flying a plane, perhaps – it seems he does not quite believe he is a real artist. 'I'm sure most artists have a much better background in art than I do – that unlike me when they were kids they used to draw a lot, and that they always had the desire to be an artist. I never even made a conscious decision to be an illustrator – it was just something that happened. I certainly can't claim that I have a great natural talent, because I don't. Some people have a natural talent for drawing, or for painting. Whatever talent I have is a matter of practise and experience, all things I've picked up as I've gone along over the years.

If there is any sort of talent inherent in me, maybe it's a sense of composition, the fact that I think in images, and there is a desire in me to create those images. That's all I know: there's always this image somewhere out there, or inside me, which I'm trying to achieve.'

Pirates of the Thunder
(New English Library, 1988)

In art college Harrison avoided attending class, confused by conflicting advice he received from different instructors. It was easier, he felt, to work things out on his own. He had enrolled in the course for graphic design but discovered he did not enjoy it much: 'The only thing I enjoyed, besides photography, was illustration – so I became an illustrator.'

But the background in graphic design has probably served him better than a less practical grounding in fine arts, versing him in the practicalities of printing, reproduction and book design. His paintings, after all, are created for a purpose and that is to adorn the cover of a book, not to hang on a wall in a museum. The look of a painting as he sees it, still lying flat on his worktable, colours fresh and unmuddied by poor reproduction, no detail obscured by lettering, is not the final product his audience will see, and that is something he is able to keep in mind when he is planning an illustration. Even so, some of his paintings have been reduced so much in size or hacked around that the original compositional sense is lost. One of the benefits of a book like this is that finally all his paintings can be seen in their original form.

Of wraparound covers, of which he has done quite a few, he says: 'They're just a publicity gimmick to help the reps get orders when they go around to the bookshops. They're not for the public at all. It's a pity because I go to all the trouble of doing a big painting and then people don't see it because the publisher puts text over it – half of it's on the back anyway, and who is ever going to flatten out a book to look at the whole picture?'

In one instance the publisher commissioned one painting which was to be divided into three covers – the painting as a whole could be viewed only by the unlikely reader able and willing to collect, flatten out and join up the covers of all three books. For that Harrison had to order an unusually long board – 'they had to bring it down in a lorry' – which protruded from each end of his desk as he worked.

In that case the special problem had been imposed by the publisher; when he came to do covers for the *Tales of the Bard* series by Michael Scott (pages 56–57, 60–63) Harrison seemed to have made things unnecessarily difficult for himself. Luckily, there was also an easy way out: 'At the time that I did the first one (*Magician's Law*) there were a lot of covers

Masks of the Masters
(New English Library, 1988)

around using panels – panels seemed to be the in-thing to use on fantasy books. I liked the idea of panels anyway, having just done something with that shape for *Eve: Her Story*, and it seemed to me to be an interesting way of breaking up the ordinary dull front cover rectangle. So, while Klimt influenced my *Eve*, that in turn influenced the cover for *Magician's Law*. But, having done all that fancy scrollwork as a frame for the portrait on the first one, I realized I really didn't want to have to keep painting the same thing again every time. So for the second in that series I painted the landscape as one painting and the skull portrait separately, as an insert. Not only does it take longer to do it the way I did the first time, but also, if someone wants to buy a painting, having the graphics on it might understandably put them off somewhat!'

Warriors of the Storm
(New English Library, 1988)

Vampire insert for
Death's Law: Tales of the Bard

Death's Law:
Tales of the Bard
(Sphere Books, 1988)

Andelain
(Dragon's World, 1982)
*'This was one of the first
fantasy landscapes I ever
painted, and it set me off
along that road. It's a picture
of the beautiful forested area
in Stephen Donaldson's*
Chronicles of Thomas
Covenant.*'*
MARK HARRISON

**Demon's Law:
Tales of the Bard**
(Sphere Books, 1987)
*'This was influenced by that wonderful
painting* The Great Day of His Wrath *by
John Martin, which I've often seen in the
Tate Gallery. That image of Armageddon,
with flames and smoke and destruction on
such a vast scale seemed just right to
illustrate a book which was about wars
to end civilization.'*
MARK HARRISON

Skull insert for
**Demon's Law:
Tales of the Bard**

Magician's Law:
Tales of the Bard
(Sphere Books, 1986)

5 FROM A DREAM TO A VIEW

THE SIGHT OF DISTANT mountains inspires awe and yearning in most of us, as do panoramic vistas, whether of cities or cloud-filled canyons. Yet this was not always the case. The Romantic revolution both reflected and inspired a sweeping change in attitude in western civilization towards the natural world. The primitive sense of awe, an awareness of landscape as something more than a neutral background, as something with a beauty and a numinous power of its own, was recovered in eighteenth-century Europe, partly in reaction to the overly mechanistic science of the day.

Twentieth-century science, dominated by concepts of quantum mechanics, the uncertainty principle and chaos theory, seems as flexible, imaginative, even as spiritual as art, and is certainly far from the mechanistic reductionism of the Age of Reason and what the great visionary artist of the late eighteenth century William Blake termed 'single vision and Newton's sleep.'

An appreciation of landscape may be a late acquisition of the Western mind, but it has taken such a firm hold that it is hard now to sympathize with the medieval poets who saw mountains as ugly warts marring the face of the earth, and the wilderness as synonymous with evil. While we might not be willing to give up any of the comforts of modern civilization, the very word 'nature' is identified with good, a source of refreshment and renewal, and it is now, as the wilderness perhaps trembles on the brink of final extinction, that its human destroyers finally recognize the beauty of the land. Everyone wants a room with a view, and private access to some unspoiled acreage.

The appeal of fantasy literature, whether set in the distant past, in an imaginary magical realm, or on another planet is perfectly expressed by a classically romantic large-scale landscape painting, with mountain ranges and sky offering plenty of scope for the play of light and shadow and shifting tones of colour, one or more snow-capped peaks rearing majestically in the distance and, with the possible exception of the odd castle or fortress, no sign of human habitation. Sometimes there are small figures in the picture if only to indicate the scale of their world, but if not, all the better as it allows the potential reader of the book to dream of the solitary possession of all that desirable space.

Year of the Unicorn
(Gollancz, 1986)

'Painting is but another word for feeling,' wrote the great
English landscape painter John Constable, and Mark Harrison
would probably agree with him. He begins work on his paintings with a feeling, whether it has come from a dream or the
book he just read, and he has then to turn that feeling into a
vision others can see.

Lord Valentine's Castle
(Bantam Books, USA, 1988)

Harrison finds it hard to explain how he works; words fail him as his paints do not. But if he could put his feelings simply and easily into words he probably wouldn't paint. 'Asking me to explain my work in words is like me asking you to draw what you write!' he exclaimed when I tried, again, to get him to verbalize his techniques.

'I don't work to any conscious, logical plan – there are just these feelings that I'm drawn to.

'What I start with is shapes, a sense of proportions in my mind. That's basically how I work. It's very vague at the start; the details come later. I know the feeling of what I'm looking for, I know what I want when I see it. The feeling I'm most interested in is something with an edge to it. If it's lush and romantic, fine, but there should also be a hint of something darker and more dangerous.

'But I always begin with the shapes. I've always worked this way, and the alarming thing, when I look back at what I was doing in art college, is to see that it was there from the start, the same things. There's the same recognizable style to all my work, only when I was beginning I didn't know what I was doing and over the years I've got better at it. I don't think I've developed at all, just improved my technique!

'My real obsession as an artist isn't jungle women, and it isn't mountain ranges – although as you can see I do a lot of them! – and it isn't even Hollywood lighting, much as I love it. My real obsession is much more basic and it's to do with composition. You can see it in paintings I did in 1975 – too clumsy to include in the book – and you can see it in my most recent cover painting, just handled in a more sophisticated, subtle way. There's something dark against something light.

'Usually, this is something dark in the foreground, often a figure, with a lighter landscape behind. And all my work is composed in layers, beginning with the foreground, and then a layer behind that, and a layer behind that, and sometimes a layer behind that. I compose it beginning at the front and going back, but when I actually paint it I start at the very, very back, and then paint in layers over it until I reach the figure (or whatever) in the foreground.'

Harrison recalls that while he was at art college he happened to see a Japanese film on television one evening. Although he can remember little else about it now he does remember the one scene which 'made me sit up and take notice. That actually started me off on a track I'm still following. It was a scene of men walking up a mountain in a mist, and the whole thing was a composition in tones of grey, going back in layers, like a series of silhouettes.' This scene remained crystallized in his mind, as powerful an influence on his work (even though it was in black and white) as one of his own dreams.

Tones and shades are of great interest to Harrison but, despite the influence of black and white photography on his recent work, he is totally committed to colour. Besides the obvious commercial reasons this preference probably has a connection with his desire to invest every painting with the emotional content which he usually describes as 'atmosphere.' Colours, it is well known, have a strong connection with emotional states and whether or not consciously acknowledged, colours do on the whole carry a freight of associations and meaning with them.

Blue predominates in many – perhaps most – of Harrison's fantasy landscapes; as the colour of choice it comes far ahead of yellows, reds or greens and this is certainly not by chance. The colours to be used are almost never specified by the art director; indeed, on one occasion Harrison recalls he was asked to avoid blue, if he could, on one series because of possible confusion with another, but 'even then I ended up by using a lot of blue, and nobody minded.'

He says he has no particular colour theory, and choses different colour schemes for different reasons, sometimes simply to try them out for himself. His particular fondness for blue is connected with a sense of happiness and a desirable atmosphere – blue skies for beautiful places, paradise as the land of eternal blue skies. 'I particularly like the way Maxfield Parrish used his rich blue in connection with a golden sunset light,' he says. 'I love that romantic light. The half-light of dusk or dawn are my favourite times of the day.'

Blue has an inevitable connection with the sky. Blue is the celestial, heavenly colour, and while some artists use the sky as little more than a backdrop – or the blank area at the top where the title will fit – Harrison's interest in painting skies

Swansdowne
(Arrow Books, 1985)
'Although the book is an historical saga about the early settlers of Tasmania, most of them convicts, I gave the cover a fantasy feel. The landscape is meant to be Tasmania but it is a very romanticized view of a real place.'
MARK HARRISON

again calls Constable to mind. Constable, who once embarked on a campaign of what he called 'skying' (painting skies and cloudscapes), believed that in landscape painting the sky was an 'organ of sentiment' and 'that landscape painter who does not make his skies a very material part of his composition neglects to avail himself of one of his greatest aids.' The sky is certainly not a subject which Harrison has ever neglected, and although he enjoys experimenting with other sky-colours – note how, using yellow, he effectively creates a golden sunset glow (page 82) and the hostility of a desert landscape (pages

88–89) – in creating a peaceful, alluring landscape with its echoes of Eden, depicting it as somewhere the reader might like to spend his spare time, a blue sky is almost essential.

The green sky of *World of Tiers Book 1* (page 86) is actually a plot element in the novel by Philip José Farmer, as are the eagles and the vanishing American Indian. But the design of that painting was, says Harrison, 'an attempt to recapture the look of a particular dream. It had the same composition, the same use of strong colours, dark areas and simple shapes.'

In speaking of the dreams which have been most inspirational to him, the colour of the sky often emerges as a key point. I mentioned earlier that the painting for *Cover Her Face* by P.D. James (page 34) was in part inspired by Harrison's

Majipoor Chronicles
(Bantam Books, USA, 1989)

dream of a 'really whacky' vividly coloured sky behind a huge old house. He also recalls another dream which he tried to paint, although he wasn't happy with the result: 'I was sitting on a hillside with someone else, and it was very late in the day. The sun was low, casting a yellow light on our faces and on the hill which was covered in brilliant red poppies. There was a thundery look to the purple-blue sky, and everything was lit by that late, low, yellow light.'

The fact that Harrison devoted time and energy to an uncommissioned painting indicates how powerfully the dream affected him. I suspect that hillside ablaze with poppies in the evening light beneath a stormy sky will turn up on a book cover one day, if it hasn't already.

OVERLEAF
The Hour of the Lily
(Arrow Books, 1987)
'The interest for me here was in trying a new colour combination of browns, blues and violets. For a change I could do some brown mountains, since the hills in Afghanistan actually are very dry and brown. It is meant to be Afghanistan, but don't go looking for that particular scene because you'll never find it!'
MARK HARRISON

Bridge of Birds
(Corgi Books, 1989)

Imrryr
(Dragon's World, 1982)

Red Omega
(Arrow Books, 1987)
'There were no aerial photographs of the Kremlin available so in addition to research I had to use quite a bit of imagination to create this night-time view of the Kremlin from the air. I was very pleased with the results. The way it was finally used on the book cover didn't do it justice.'
MARK HARRISON

A Noose of Light
(Futura, 1985)

The Sultan's Turret
(Futura, 1986)

The City, Not Long After
(Bantam Books, USA, 1988)

The Dragonbone Chair
(Arrow Books, 1989)
*'I had a major compositional problem with this one: they
wanted me to put the Green Angel Tower (from the story) in
the foreground, with an absolutely huge landscape, virtually
like a map, spread out below. It's a preposterous perspective,
no tower could possibly be that high! In the end they didn't
use my painting because they were afraid it would clash
with another strong yellow cover due out the same month.'*
Mark Harrison

Right **Saints** (Hatrack River, USA, 1987)

Valentine Pontifex
(Bantam Books, USA, 1989)

World of Tiers Book 1
(Sphere Books, 1986)

World of Tiers Book 2
(Sphere Books, 1986)

Into the Out Of
(New English Library, 1986)

OVERLEAF **Nature Hide and Seek: Oceans**
(Matthew Price, 1984)
'This was for a children's book about how animals camouflage themselves in their environments. It's an early example of my experiments with techniques of creating texture to give a painting more visual interest.'
MARK HARRISON

6 ADVENTURES ELSEWHERE

ALTHOUGH HE NEVER set out to specialize in one genre, it is as a fantasy illustrator that Harrison has really made his mark. 'I like doing fantasy landscapes,' he admits. 'It's satisfying to create a world, an idyllic setting, something that never existed which you can make look as if it exists. Occasionally I will put in bits from reference photographs, a lot of which I've taken myself on my travels, but it doesn't do to use anything too specific or people might recognize it – "Hey, that's not from an alien civilization, that's a pagoda in Bangkok!" Also, working from reference slows you down.'

He got into fantasy illustration in much the same way as he got into illustration in general: it just happened, with never a moment when he made a conscious decision. And while he does enjoy it, he is emphatic that he would hate to be trapped by a speciality: 'I'd go mad if every book cover I had to do was a fantasy landscape with one little figure in it.'

His influences, he suspects, are 'the same as everybody else's. I'm sure we've all looked at the same stuff, because there are quite a few artists working in the same way in the fantasy field. We've all been looking at the work of Albert Bierstadt, and the rest of the Hudson River School of artists. And then there's the Flemish landscapes, with a lot of dark, shadowy areas. I'm sure I'm not the only one to be influenced by the lush, exotic style of the Orientalists and Victorian painters like Lord Leighton and Grimshaw and Alma-Tadema, the Pre-Raphaelites, the Symbolists, and a fellow called Jean-Leon Gerome who created wonderfully languid exotic scenes. And I know we've all been looking at Maxfield Parrish, that very popular American romantic artist. Some people actually copy him, which I don't, but he is a very big influence on me, particularly in his use of sunset light and the way the yellowy-orange reflected in the skin-tones of a foreground figure sets off the blue background.' The colours and lighting favoured by Maxfield Parrish are an obvious influence in some of Harrison's most recent work, including the cover to *The Gate to Women's Country* (pages 18–19).

'I'm not a great fantasy reader; for me the books are an excuse, a way of creating atmosphere through a strange landscape, and to try out different lighting ideas. Maybe fantasy lends itself particularly well to my type of exotic romanticism,' he says.

RIGHT **Voyage to the City of the Dead**
(New English Library, 1986)

OVERLEAF **The Story of the Stone**
(Bantam Books, 1987)
'Undoubtedly my most popular cover – it was even nominated for an award. I spent a lot of time worrying about this one because it was my first American commission. I had to keep reminding myself that they had hired me because they liked my work, so all I had to do was what I normally did, instead of making it too hard on myself. The positive response in the end was really gratifying.'
MARK HARRISON

Asked to describe his ideal commission he says, with a laugh, 'My own book cover! That was the painting I was waiting to do. Other than that, I have to say that it's an almost unconscious process for me most of the time. I don't really know what I want to do until I do it. My ideal job is one that pays well, that I enjoy doing and manage to create something successful, and then this is recognized by the art director, and the author says what a good job I did, and then the fan mail comes in, and I get nominated for an award . . .'

His cover for *The Story of the Stone* by Barry Hughart (page 94–95) seems to fulfil his criteria – although it did not win, it was in fact nominated for the Chesley, an award presented annually by the American Association of Science Fiction and Fantasy Artists. Harrison agrees: 'That was rather like an ideal job, to an extent. It was the first commission I had from America, and it was bought for the hardback, then also used on the paperback, then for both English editions, then on the German hardback and paperback, and then I sold the original artwork to a doctor in Marietta, Georgia . . .'

His brief was for a Chinese landscape, a valley with figures in the foreground walking toward a split mountain. 'So I got out some references and looked at pictures of Chinese mountains, and the idea came to me very quickly. It was pretty obvious, because the Kweilin Hills are such marvellous shapes that you just have to use them, shapes like that. Except that I didn't, because there aren't any hills that look like the ones I've painted! What I did was take the idea of those wonderful, sugarloaf mountain shapes in my head, and then I picked up the brush and made a mark, and then made another mark and just saw what the brush did, just let it come out making up the landscape as I went along. Then I took photographs of a friend in different costumes for the figures. The flower had to be in the picture because it's part of the story, along with this weird stone – I really think the picture would be better without it, but it had to be there.'

Despite his recent success, Harrison is not worried that by making something of a name for himself as a fantasy illustrator he would be trapped into being asked to do the same kind of covers again and again. 'I think it's up to the illustrator, that if you want to do something different you just have to fit it in somehow. Fit it into the painting and it will be noticed and

Decision at Doona
(Corgi Books, 1990)
'Recently I have been trying out more interesting lighting effects. Here, instead of the usual undifferentiated lighting of most of my landscapes, I tried to use 'Hollywood lighting' as if it were a stage set and huge lamps had been brought in to light it for a film.'
MARK HARRISON

another direction will develop from there. Anyway, although there is definitely a genre of fantasy landscapes around at the moment I think it's coming to an end. The idea has been over-used. I think people are getting tired of the pure fantasy land-scape and are looking more towards figurative work.'

For years, feeling that his figurative work was his weak point, Harrison concentrated on landscapes and still-life com-positions. In the past few years, however, he has been making the effort to improve his figure painting and now he seems to be trying to forge a synthesis between these two types of painting. Earlier forays in this direction can be detected in the series of covers he did for the P.D. James novels (pages 28 and 29, 31–35) in which he decided to combine the foreground still-life composition with an atmospheric background, and also in some of the 'jungle women' covers in which the land-scape creeps forward to become living decoration for the cen-tral female figure. But what he is trying to do now is a bit different and much more conscious.

After so many years of following a career which he implies 'just happened,' and despite his habit of working instinctively without a conscious plan, Mark Harrison came to a time when he was ready to assess his career, and make his own choices. Now, rather than simply agreeing to whatever comes along, he admits that he has a conscious 'master plan.'

'I was never very good at figures, that was always my weak point as an artist, so I tended to be quite happy that I could do a lot of landscapes. I understand that some illustrators can actually do figure drawing from life, but most of us can't, so we have to take photographs. Maybe I was a bit lazy in the past, and that's partly my own fault, but now that I'm getting more money from America I can afford to spend more time on each job, I can afford to hire my own models – also, my own standards are higher now, so I will spend the time and effort.

'Lately, in my dreams, I've been seeing landscapes with figures. The two have come together, and now I'm trying to reflect that element of my dreams in my work. I am determined to improve my figure painting so that I can finally paint these pictures I know are in me somewhere. Luckily, I've got a vision of what I want. It doesn't always happen, but this time I know what I'm aiming for.'

On the Seas of Destiny
(Headline Books, 1989)

The Ivanhoe Gambit
(Headline Books, 1987)

Legend
(Arrow Books, 1988)
*'That may look like a
legendary hero from the
distant past but really it's
Wayne, a big, muscular bloke
dressed up like some Northern
barbarian. At the time he was
wielding a sword in a
Brighton back garden while I
took reference photographs.
The neighbours peered out
behind their curtains and
wondered what it was all
about!'*
MARK HARRISON

The King Beyond the Gate
(Arrow Books, 1988)

Ghost King
(Arrow Books, 1988)

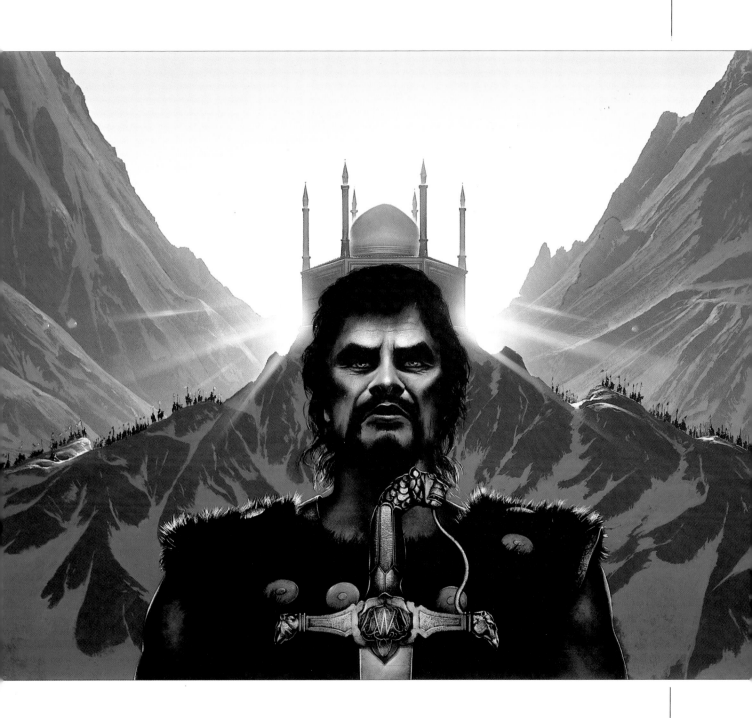

A Wolf in Shadow
(Arrow Books, 1988)

**The Last Sword
of Power**
(Arrow Books, 1988)
*'Maybe someday I'll put
myself in a picture, but this
isn't it. The sinister ogre here
is my mate Paul standing on
top of his sofa wrapped in a
dressing gown and pretending
to row a boat with his broom.
The things friends will do to
help out an artist!'*
MARK HARRISON

LEFT **The Broken Wheel**
(New English Library, 1989)

ABOVE **The Middle Kingdom**
(New English Library, 1988)

Black Trillium
(Bantam Books, USA, 1989)
*'To my mind an evil tower
ought to be black but this one,
according to the book, had to
be white. I found it very
difficult to make the snowy
landscape look unpleasant
and threatening enough. I've
probably made it look just a
little too pretty. Maybe I'm not
suited to depicting something
completely evil.'*
MARK HARRISON

The Call of the Sword
(Headline Books, 1987)

The Waking of Orthlund
(Headline Books, 1989)

PREVIOUS SPREAD
Seventh Son
(Arrow Books, 1988)
'I'm not very good at painting children so naturally for the paperback they focused right in on the figure of the child! What I like is the mellow New England autumnal atmosphere. The tree was obviously inspired by Maxfield Parrish; the mill in the background is a real one.'
Mark Harrison

Ecotopia
(Bantam Books, USA, 1989)

The Fall of Fyorlund
(Headline Books, 1989)

Into Narsindal
(Headline Books, 1990)

LEFT **In the Caves
of Exile**
(Headline Books, 1988)

RIGHT **Walkabout Woman**
(Bantam Books, USA, 1988)

BELOW **Wyvern**
(Harper & Row, USA, 1988)

PREVIOUS PAGE **Lyonesse**
(Dragon's World, 1982)
*'When I look at this I realize I
don't always improve with
practice. This early tidal wave
works a lot better than the one
I did this year as the cover for
a* Hawklan *novel (page 119).
It is difficult to achieve a still
scene with the sense of
something horrendous about
to happen.'*
MARK HARRISON

Project Pendulum
(Bantam Books, USA, 1988)

Grass
(Corgi Books, 1990)
*'I really did enjoy painting
this. Of course I enjoy them
all or I wouldn't do them, but
in this one I particularly love
the wild colours and the
lighting; it has a real dream-
like feel to it, at least to me. I
always try for that feeling, but
it's not often that I can point
to a picture and say: that's
what a dream looks like. This
is one of them.'*
MARK HARRISON

ACKNOWLEDGEMENTS

Mark Harrison would like to thank Jamie Warren, Liz
Laczynjka and Peter Cotton for help and encouragement,
Matthew Price for the use of the *Ocean Life* cover, Nadia Ariova
for modelling, and Steve and Sally for the inspiration.